KNIGHTS
Through the Ages

R.T. Watts

Teacher Notes:

This story explores the many and varied roles of a knight in the Middle Ages, and how kingdoms operated in these times. Students will learn about their training, their weapons, their armour and their responsibilities as they fought to serve their ruler and protect their kingdom from invaders. Comparisons can be made regarding the importance of knights in the Middle Ages compared to those of today.

Discussion points for consideration:

1. Knights seemed to have a much more important and dangerous role back in the Middle Ages than the knights of today. Discuss the differences.

2. Vast differences exist between how countries operate today and how kingdoms operated in the Middle Ages. List some of these.

3. Discuss the different kinds of knights that existed in the Middle Ages and how they rose through the ranks to become a knight.

4. Why did knights become obsolete?

Sight words, difficult to decode words, and infrequent words to be introduced and practiced before reading this book:

knights, Templar, century, squire, armour, United Kingdom, British Government, Honors System, rebellion, politicians, expensive, equipment, pilgrims, crusaders, Palestine, medicines, infections, dysentery, religious, ceremony, kilometres, rescue, information, understanding.

Contents

1. What are Knights?

The King of the United Kingdom can still make you a knight. You need to do something very special for the United Kingdom and then you get the title of "Sir" if a man, or "Dame" if a woman.

Knights aren't just people in suits of metal armor. They are still around today. What did these knights do?

Olivia Newton-John became Dame Olivia Newton-John. Men who are made a knight are called "Sir". Sir Frank Lowy is an Australian knight. It is now called the Honors System.

People can still be knighted today for good work done for the United Kingdom. How did this start? Knights have been around for a long time. If you were in control of a country, you needed friends. The ruler of the country needed to have people around him or her, who would support them, and even fight for them. If you had no support, then off you went to the chopping block!

The ruler of the land was keen to keep as many people happy as possible. The ruler needed an army to fight off invaders, and a lot of people who were loyal to help you keep power.

5

The knight was the name given to men of the warrior class. Knights were below the nobles but above the peasants.

The ruler used a system of titles to make sure he had a lot of people who were friends and supporters. If a fight for the rule of the country broke out, it was stopped if the ruler stayed in control. A rebellion would only work if enough of the knights and nobles changed sides.

When this happened, the ruler lost power and was overthrown.

Who's Who of Power

King

Nobles/Bishops

Knights/Gentry

Commoners/Peasants

The knight lived off the rent from land given to him by the ruler. He was trained to fight using swords and other weapons. The knight had to be able to ride a horse into battle.

If a war was started by the king, prince or a noble, then the knight was called on to fight. The knight was like a security guard who had to fight for the ruler. The knight lived at his home when not doing battles or work for the ruler.

As part of this deal, land was given to the knight. This land could be used for animals and crops. The peasants and farmers who rented land from him would farm the crops and look after the animals.

There were kingdoms all over Europe. These were not countries like today. Countries today have politicians and governments. The kings and queens today have little power. They are there as part of the culture.

This video outlines the current kings and queens of Europe.

In the Middle Ages, things were very different. The king ruled over the land and had almost complete control. Anyone who got in their way was in big trouble! Total control took all their time.

They had to be careful of a takeover at any time. There were a lot of people who wanted the job of king. To make sure they were safe from being kicked out or killed, a ruler would need to build a support group. This group of dukes, princes, barons and knights wanted to keep what they had. To do this, they needed to have their own army they could use to support the ruler.

This support group had to supply archers, foot soldiers and horses. If the king was attacked they had to defend him. It was simple – if you want all the land and good things you have to help protect the ruler.

Knights needed many skills and expensive equipment and horses. They also had to be good fighters and horsemen.

To do well in a battle you had to have good gear. This gear included armor, swords, lances and other weapons. You needed to have archers to fire a lot of arrows as well as soldiers on foot. Horses had to be trained for battle. You also needed to train to make sure you were ready for the battles.

If they were successful in a battle, they could be given a house with land and workers. The knight was a soldier for the nobles and kings. Scan this code for a link to knights in battle.

2. Castles

Europe was a different place compared to how it is now. People didn't build castles just to show they were a big shot. The castle was the last line of defence. If you got attacked by bandits, you ran to the castle. You closed the doors and were ready to fight off the attack.

All the village people would rush inside, and the castle gates would be locked. Inside, the archers and soldiers would start firing on the attackers. It was very difficult to attack a castle. The open ground meant you could be hit by rocks or arrows.

It was hard to control all of the lands. The woods were filled with bandits, wolves, bears and lawless people. Roads were footpaths, not highways. People walked between towns. In the towns it may be safe from bandits, but it was a scary time. You had to know where you were going and who was looking after you.

People could be killed on a simple walk in the country. People were very scared and most were happy to have knights and an important man with a castle to look after them. This was the deal: everyone got looked after and the knights got land and money.

3. The Knights Templar

In the Middle Ages you needed to have protection. You had to have people to do the fighting. To attack the bad people and fierce animals you had to have knights. There were knights all over Europe.

In France, Portugal, Spain and the Holy Land, the knights grouped together and looked after long trails. They stopped robbers and bandits. To do this they asked for payment to use the pathways. The knights had castles and safe houses for the people walking as pilgrims. The knights became rich. Even the pope was fed up with these knights becoming too powerful. He decided to get rid of them.

These knights were called the Knights Templar. They were a cross between a monk and a knight. These knights were so powerful they took over a lot of Spain, Portugal and France. They built churches and castles along the pilgrim trails and charged people to use these trails. You had no choice but to pay.

The Knights Templar was known because of the cross on his front cloth. The Knights Templar began as Crusaders to the Holy Land in Palestine. The King of France owed a lot of money to the Knights Templar. His plan was to torture and burn them at the stake. This was a bad end to their story!

4. Becoming a Knight

So who can make you a knight? In Europe during the Middle Ages it was the head of state. This could be the King or Queen, nobles or maybe the Pope.

They would give people their knighthood. People were usually knighted for fighting in wars. Later it could also be for other services to the ruler, church, or country.

A knighthood was first given to the men who did battle on horseback. These were the toughest warriors. To become a knight was a big honor and it was very important. Knights were usually paid with land.

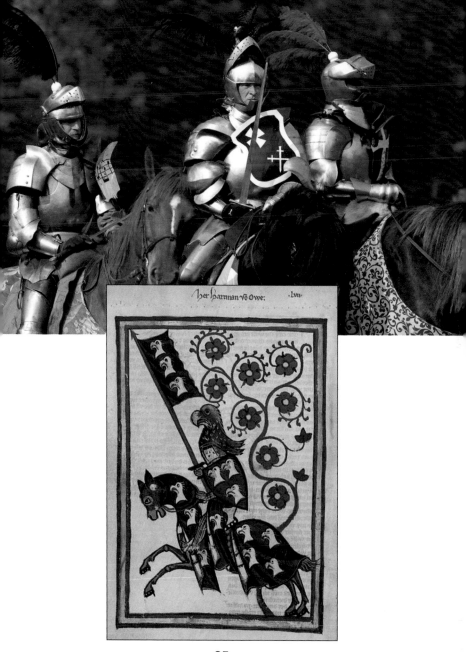

The knight could fight on foot, from a castle, or a ship, but most importantly they fought on horseback. Knights were great horsemen. Horses were fast and gave them the element of surprise. Horsemen could beat soldiers on foot. They could quickly break through enemy forces.

It took a lot of hard work to train to be a knight on horseback. You began your training when you were very young. You rode horses all the time and then started to practice fighting moves.

5. Knights in the 11th Century

The knight in the 11th Century had a shield made of wood and leather. The shield was there to stop the blows from axes and swords. The sword was long and broad and could pierce and slash.

The armor was mail on the body and a helmet on his head. The helmet point made swords bounce off.

6. 12th Century Weapons

Different weapons had different uses in a fight.

Some common weapons were:

a/ swords - these were used for stabbing and slashing.

b/ mace - these were blunt smashing weapons to crush and break armor.

c/ lance - these were long weapons which could be used on a horse.

d/ battle axe - these were used to hack through enemies' helmet or mail.

 This is a link to more information on weapons.

7. Death and Disease

Fighting was a deadly business. The death rate was very high. In battles, the numbers killed or seriously hurt were huge.

Wounds and broken bones were painful and hard to heal. Cuts and wounds were not treated with medicines to stop infections.

The big killer was not the enemy but disease. The worst disease was dysentery. This was a disease of the stomach. This caused the knight to lose all their water and then bleed internally. All their organs started to fail. It killed a lot more soldiers than the enemy.

8. 13th Century Armor

By the 13th Century, armor had changed again. The head was protected with a full helmet. This covered the whole head and had a slit to see through. This meant they gave up full vision to protect the face.

The weapon being used was a large and heavy axe. If the sword or dagger could not cut the armor then a heavy axe could smash it. The axe would smash the helmet and skull causing death.

A shield was still used to fend off heavy blows from this crushing weapon.

9. 14th Century Armor

By the 14th Century, the knight had more steel plates. The metalsmiths had become better and steel was being shaped carefully. Full body armor was being made.

The plates of steel could stop heavy weapons and swords. The knight could carry a smaller shield and a smaller weapon for punching holes in the steel.

The head was totally covered with a helmet. The flip up face visor was used to see better when they didn't need to protect their face.

10. The Page

Knights started their training early in life. A knight was born as a noble or the son of a knight.

Training to be a knight started at seven years old. The name given to a young knight in training was a page.

The page's job was to follow the knight and look after his equipment. They would also go hunting with falcons. They had to study with religious people.

Pages looked after older knights in battle by cleaning their armor and looking after the horses. They would go with the knights to battles and on foreign journeys.

Watch how a knight would get his full body armor put on. This explains what the metal armor was meant to do.

The full metal armor was getting complex. Better armor was being made by the metalsmiths.

As guns were invented and got better the knight in armor was no longer a part of an army.

11. The Squire

As the page got older he was instructed in sword fighting, riding horses, manners and how to act as a knight in warfare and using combat weapons.

After the page turned fifteen, they became a squire. A ceremony was held by the priest.

The squire was trained to use armor and weapons as well as other skills such as dancing! All this training was done while wearing heavy armor, including the dancing!

12. The Last Knights in Armor

Countries were getting big full-time armies together and the knights were not needed as much.

People had guns that could punch through steel armor. A gunshot from one soldier could kill a knight.

By the 17th Century there were big armies, and most had guns. The knight was an expensive way to put together an army of fighting people.

Knights went into the armies as officers. Many of the links were kept but the days of doing battle with swords and steel armor were gone. They had tanks instead of armor, and guns instead of swords.

Word Bank

crusades	pilgrims
armor	Palestine
medicine	dysentery
unnecessary	religious
expensive	rebellion
knights	United Kingdom
infections	century
Templar	squire
swords	ceremony
firearms	countries
officers	equipment